Hunting Red

Written by Jean Snodgress Wiedenheft

Illustrated by Gabrielle Anderson

Pocket Mouse Publishing
Cedar Rapids, Iowa

Introduction

    Each picture on the following pages was inspired by the Indian Creek Nature Center in Cedar Rapids, Iowa. Visit, and you may find the sycamore tree still gracing the banks of Indian Creek and the sugar maple still sustaining yellow-bellied sapsuckers. Or, you may not. A strong wind can topple the largest oak tree, and a tiny ant can return a dead tree to the soil. The composition of the flora and fauna changes with the seasons, with the weather patterns, and with human management.

    In the spring, snow trilliums and pussy willows bloom. Red-winged blackbirds and warblers return from the south. During the summer, monarch caterpillars munch the leaves of the milkweeds and hummingbirds nest in the tree canopy. By fall, the bright red berry clusters of the green dragon are splashed throughout the woods, tucked under the white sprigs of blooming snake root. In winter, juncos flock along the forest edge and otters create slides into Indian Creek. No matter when you visit, every journey you make through this magical, wild place will be different.

www.pocketmousepublishing.com

Dedicated to Jerry and Aria

giant leopard moth caterpillar, giant leopard moth

My brother and I are sitting in the prairie crab apple tree when he asks me, "Is red still your favorite color?"

Hunting Red

Copyright © 2014 by Jean Snodgress Wiedenheft

Published by Pocket Mouse Publishing

All rights reserved. No part of this book may be reproduced or utilized in any form or by any means, electronic or mechanical, including photocopying, recording, or by any information storage or retrieval system, without permission in writing from the publisher.

Inquiries should be sent to:
pocketmousepublishing@gmail.com

ISBN-13: 978-0615907925

I'm not actually sure.

The mug I drink
hot chocolate
from is purple,
the color of the night sky just
after sunset.

My bedroom is the color of a
robin's egg.

I never wear red. I don't even
have a red scarf.

land snail, American robin, robin nest, black walnut tree

I usually wear brown. There are many different shades to choose from.

My favorite is the rich sable of the brown mink.

The mink's coat camouflages him, helping him hide under bushes and blend in with the ground.

Wearing brown helps me blend in with my surroundings, too.

rose hips, brown mink, wild rose bush

 I can't fit under bushes. Instead I sit against the trunk of a dead tree.

Then, if I am quiet, I can see who is wearing red. If I move too much, the crows will see me.

When crows spot me, they start cawing and don't stop. It alerts the whole forest that there is a stranger nearby.

Other animals know to hide.

leafhopper, American crow, snag

I try to remember
that sitting very
still is important.

I hunt with my eyes for a
bright, brilliant red.

I'm not looking for orange,
which is sometimes called red.

I'm not looking for the orange
of the red fox.

*russula mushroom, fiddlehead fern,
limestone crevice, wild ginger, red fox*

I am looking for
the yellow-bellied
sapsucker.

The sapsucker's yellow belly
is so pale I seldom see it,
and he doesn't actually suck sap.

I don't always find the sapsucker,
but I can find where he has been. He
drills tiny holes in straight lines across
the bark of trees.

When the sap seeps out of the holes,
insects come to drink it. Then the
sapsucker comes back to eat the bugs.

maple seed, sugar maple tree, yellow-bellied sapsucker

Sometimes to find
red I just have to
find the right plant.

If I watch a columbine, a
ruby-throated hummingbird
is bound to fly by.

His wings beat so fast
I often can't see his
sparkling iridescent throat
until he hovers
to drink the nectar.

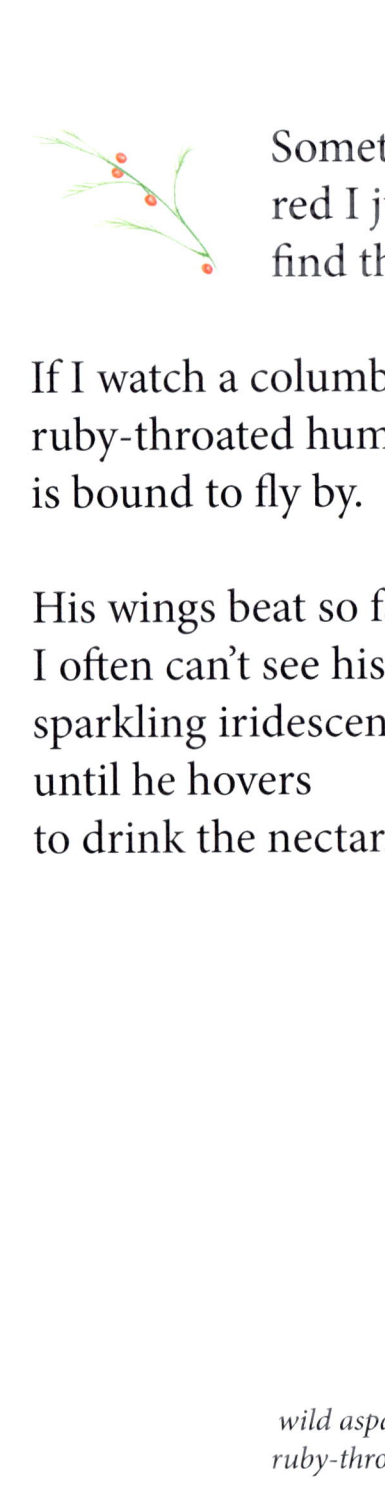

*wild asparagus, columbine,
ruby-throated hummingbird*

 The hardest red to
find in the forest
is the scarlet cup.

Since this mushroom
is only the size of a
chocolate chip,
I have to look
very, very carefully.

They peek out amidst the soil
and the sticks.

*rose-breasted grosbeak, scarlet cups,
artist's conk, white-footed deer mouse*

 The pileated woodpecker is enormous.

Even when I don't see him, I can hear him drumming on trees deep in the forest.

He is such a striking bird that when I do see him I always want to say,

"Did you see that?"

In the forest where most animals try to stay hidden, the pileated woodpecker is not afraid to be seen.

green dragon berries, white oak, pileated woodpecker

 I do not always have
to go so far into the
forest to find red.

The cardinals do not mind
if I sit outside with them.

They flit about as if
I were not there,
calling to each other
with a long, piercing whistle.

I wish I could whistle like that.

The females are not a real red, but
the males are bright and bold. They
even have red beaks.

bur oak acorns, American cardinal, oak-hickory savanna

 Not all of the birds can
live in the cold winter,
with the blowing wind
and snow and ice.

Many songbirds migrate south,
where the insects and seeds
remain plentiful.

In the spring,
scarlet tanagers return
and are easy to spot.

All I have to do is visit
the mulberry tree.

*mulberry leaf and berry, cup plant (yellow), scarlet tanager,
mulberry tree, purple coneflower, butterfly weed (orange)*

Even in the summer,
I still wear brown.
The tree leaves
camouflage everything, making
it harder to hunt red.

Birds are being more secretive,
protecting their nests and families.

But there is still red to be found if I head
to the meadow. Not just any meadow
will do.

I need a tallgrass prairie, where the
plants grow taller than I am, where the
animals have many places to hide, and
where there are too many flowers to
count.

garter snake, big bluestem, cup plant, purple coneflower

 There are two ways to walk through a prairie.

Sometimes I just wind through the different clumps of grasses. It's a tough walk.

Other times I find a trail that animals have made, and I follow that path.

Every time the grasses get stepped on, it becomes easier to walk that way again.

I like to think about animals finding my path and following me.

Indian paintbrush, big bluestem, Indian grass (tan), cup plant, yellow coneflower, rattlesnake master (brown), lead plant (purple)

Hunting red in the prairie
is different than waiting for
a bird to fly by.

Plants tend to stay put,
unless they get picked.

Once I find a cardinal flower,
I can keep going back
to the same place,
making my own path.

The cardinal flower is
the same color as the bird.
It stands out brilliantly
against the tans and greens
of the grasses.

*great blue lobelia,
cardinal flower, summer azure butterfly*

 Then I hike uphill to the sand prairie, where the plants grow sparsely.

I wear my shoes, because prickly pear cacti grow in the sandy soil. I like that the cactus lives here, even though it is far from the desert.

I am hunting the royal catchfly flower.

The flower doesn't look big enough to catch a fly, but it is sticky enough to snag them.

I have seen the royal catchfly trap gnats and sweat bees.

sweat bee, purple prairie clover, bush clover (brown), royal catchfly (red), partridge pea (yellow), sand love grass, prickly pear cactus

"Yes," I say to my brother, from the branches of the sycamore tree. "Red is absolutely, positively my favorite color."

Then I ask, "What's your favorite color?"

Behind the Scenes

The cover: Red-tailed hawks are year-round residents at the Indian Creek Nature Center. The hawk's tail is more orange than red, but it is striking in the sunlight. This is an easy bird to identify as it glides on thermals and hunts for mice, snakes, and other small animals.

The crab apple tree: Prairie crab apples are Iowa's only native apple tree. The native crab apple tree is covered in spines and produces hard, sour apples. The fruit is edible, and enjoyed by mammals and birds. Crab apple jelly is delicious.

The sand prairie: One hundred and fifty years ago, the Nature Center's sand prairie was part of a much larger prairie. Fifteen years ago, it was a soybean field. Today, it is being restored to prairie once again.

The sycamore tree: Sycamore trees can grow to enormous sizes in the river bottoms and lowlands. This one stands along Indian Creek. Sycamore bark is smooth and mottled white, creating a ghostly appearance in the moonlight. Sycamore leaves can be larger than this page, and the seeds and twigs often litter the forest floor.

The artist: Artist Gabrielle Anderson spent the summer of 2012 volunteering at the Indian Creek Nature Center, helping restore the prairies and woodlands. She was fascinated by the depth of color and detail the natural world reveals when you immerse yourself in it. Gabrielle studies environmental science and horticulture in Virginia, where she lives with her brindle Akita, Tenshi.

The author: As the Land Steward of the Indian Creek Nature Center, author Jean Snodgress Wiedenheft works to create natural, healthy habitats that enable wildlife to thrive and for visitors to explore. She has a BS in journalism and mass communication from Iowa State University. Jean lives outside of Cedar Rapids, Iowa, with her black Labrador, Nitro.

The place: Indian Creek Nature Center is a private, nonprofit organization that manages 300 acres of land in eastern Iowa. It is a place anyone can explore, learn about sustainability, and enjoy nature. Visit www.indiancreeknaturecenter.org to learn about programs, get involved as a volunteer, make a donation, or download a trail map to begin your adventure.

sycamore flower, sycamore seedpod